Monsters
and Mythical Creatures

Demons

Kris Hirschmann

ReferencePoint
Press®

San Diego, CA

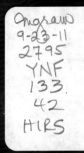

ReferencePoint Press®

© 2011 ReferencePoint Press, Inc.
Printed in the United States

For more information, contact:
ReferencePoint Press, Inc.
PO Box 27779
San Diego, CA 92198
www. ReferencePointPress.com

LIBRARY OF CONGRESS CATALOGING-IN-PUBLICATION DATA

Hirschmann, Kris, 1967–
  Demons / by Kris Hirschmann.
    p. cm. — (Monsters and mythical creatures)
  Includes bibliographical references and index.
  ISBN-13: 978-1-60152-147-7 (hardback)
  ISBN-10: 1-60152-147-2 (hardback)
  1. Demonology. I. Title.
  BF1531.H57 2011
  133.4'2—dc22
                                                    2010029905

Contents

What Is a Demon?

In the middle of the night, a woman named Ann Haywood started awake. She looked toward her bedroom window. There, explains in a book called *The Demon Syndrome*, she saw a terrifying figure:

It was clothed in a black flowing shroud with two arms and hands extending from the edges . . . but they were not human appendages. Not normal, regular arms and hands, but cloven ones like those of a pig. The teeth and mouth seemed inhuman. Four fangs protruded where incisors should have been, and rough, thornlike projections were the closest semblance of human teeth. Its face had an almond shape and the skin was tinted pink. But it was the eyes that frightened Ann most, for they burned crimson. . . . The creature had only a small amount of wiry hair that stood straight up, and the ears were pointed . . . there were no feet . . . the thing moved by gliding and floating.[1]

Did You Know?

Some people believe that the beings identified as demons are actually aliens. These aliens live secretly on Earth and try constantly to lead humans astray.

This being was definitely up to no good. In later interviews, Ann explained that the creature wanted to steal her soul and devour her human body. It almost succeeded, at one point covering Ann's face with its sticky, spike-filled mouth. It was forced to give up, however, when Ann invoked the name of God. The monster fled through the bedroom wall and disappeared into the night, never to bother Ann again.

Ann's story offers a classic description of a demon—an evil being that is said to exist outside the human realm. These entities are

Demons—many with fanglike teeth, crimson eyes, and pointed ears—descend on unsuspecting victims, some say, in search of souls to steal and bodies to devour.

Over the ages people have tried many ways of appeasing demons, including giving sacrificial offerings. Rituals involving the sacrifice of animals continue in some places today, as can be seen in this 2008 photograph of a ritualistic killing of a buffalo calf in India.

usually described as being ugly, strong, and unpredictable. Most of all, however, they are dangerous. Demons wish ill upon humans, and they have the power to make this wish come true. They can frighten or hurt people. They can convince people to commit murder or other heinous acts. They can possess people's bodies and minds. In extreme cases, demons can even kill their human victims.

It is no wonder, considering demons' destructive potential, that humans always have feared these entities. They also have found many ways to fight them. Historical records show that people have tried to appease demons through sacrifices

Did You Know?

People who study demons are called demonologists. People who worship demons are called demonolators.

and offerings. They have sought to conquer demons through prayer and faith. They even have appointed human mystics to bargain with angry entities. Depending on the belief system, any or all of these techniques have been said to deter demonic attack.

But no technique can entirely dispel demons. No matter how many times these beings are cast out, they always seem to return. This fact is discouraging but perhaps not surprising. Religious scholars say that evil is part of the human condition. Demons, whether they are real or imaginary, allow people to put a face on this evil. These entities therefore have an important place in the natural order. As long as humans do bad things, demons will continue to exist—or at least to take the blame for humankind's many misfortunes.

Chapter 1

Demons in World Mythology

A variation of the word "demon" first appeared in the writings of ancient Greece. Spelled *daimon*, the word referred to supernatural beings that ranked somewhere between mortals and gods. These beings had individual personalities and could be either good or bad. They were much like people in their thoughts and actions.

The demons of other traditions, unfortunately, were not always so benign. Nasty or downright evil entities have existed in just about every era, culture, and belief system. Supernaturally scary, these creatures have spawned countless tales of temptation, destruction, and horror.

The Earliest Demons

The earliest known demon lore comes from ancient Mesopotamia. This region was located between the Tigris and Euphrates rivers, within the borders of present-day Iraq. From about 3500 B.C. to 500 B.C., Mesopotamia was home to the Sumerian, Babylonian, and Judean peoples. Demons were a constant concern in all of these cultures.

In the Mesopotamian belief system, demons were considered to be the spirits of natural forces such as fire, plagues, and other misfortunes. They were everywhere, and they were constantly trying to harm people. To stave off demonic attacks, people used amulets and other magical deterrents. One source explains a specific technique: "They placed special bowls inscribed with potent word charms upside down under the foundations of their houses to catch demons and prevent them from entering the houses through the ground."[2]

Lamashtu was perhaps the most feared Mesopotamian demon. The daughter of the sky god Anu, Lamashtu had a hairy body and a lioness's head. She also had long, sharp fingernails and birdlike feet with terrible talons. She was usually shown standing on a donkey's back, carrying a double-headed serpent in each hand.

Lamashtu's behavior was just as scary as her appearance. This demon preyed on unborn babies, snatching them out of their mother's wombs to gnaw on their bones. Lamashtu was also said to kidnap infants while they were breastfeeding. She would whisk the helpless children away and suck the blood from their tiny bodies.

As vicious as these deeds were, they were only the start of Lamashtu's awful activities. When she was not eating babies, Lamashtu brought nightmares and diseases to humans everywhere. She killed plants and infested rivers and streams. If she was in an especially bad mood, Lamashtu sometimes even slaughtered adults just for fun.

To protect themselves against Lamashtu, the ancient Mesopotamians sometimes called upon another vicious demon named Pazuzu. Pazuzu was the king of the wind demons. Associated especially with cold northwesterly winds, Pazuzu brought storms, droughts, and locusts. He was angry, malevolent, and dangerous. But these qualities could be very helpful to humans. Pazuzu was so jealous of his territory that he drove all other demons away. He particularly hated Lamashtu and spent a great deal of time fighting with her. Amulets featuring images of the fearsome Pazuzu, therefore, were popular adornments in ancient Mesopotamia.

Did You Know?

In 2009 the residents of an Indian town built and burned a 175-foot (53.3m) effigy of the demon Ravana. The effigy weighed about 6,600 pounds (3,000kg) and contained enough bamboo sticks to build nearly 50 huts.

Hindu Demons

The Hindus of ancient India had plenty of demons to worry about, too. Hinduism recognized many categories of unpleasant spirits, including the Asuras or "anti-gods," the cannibalistic Rakshasas, the ghostly Bhuta, and others. In one passage, a sacred Hindu text called the Bhagavad Gita collectively describes these beings as follows: "Those of demonic nature know not what to do or refrain from; Purity is not found in them, nor is good conduct, nor is truth. . . . These ruined souls, small-minded and of cruel deeds, arise as the enemies of the world, bent on its destruction. Filled with insatiable desires, full of hypocrisy, pride, and arrogance, holding evil thoughts through delusion, they foully work."[3]

Part of this "foul work" involved people. Hindu demons sometimes brought conflict and disease into the human realm. They were also known to toy with mortals. A class of demons called Yakshas, for instance, loved to disguise themselves as beautiful women and tempt human men into the deep woods. The Yakshas would then turn into trees, leaving their victims alone and hopelessly lost.

Other demons caused most of their trouble in the divine realm. The Rakshasas were especially well known for stirring up problems of this type. One popular tale recounts the story of Ravana, the

The class of demons known as Yakshas (pictured in this ancient cave painting found in China) like to toy with mortals by disguising themselves as beautiful women and then luring men into the woods. Once there, the Yakshas transform into trees and the men become hopelessly lost.

leader of the Rakshasas. Ravana was a fearsome specimen with 10 heads, 20 arms, and gigantic fangs. This demon king kidnapped Sita, the wife of the god Rama. He held Sita hostage until her husband arrived with an army of gods by his side. After a long battle, Rama defeated Ravana, and Sita was finally free to return to her husband's home.

Today, the demon Ravana is considered a symbol of evil in most parts of India. His effigy is even burned on certain festival days. In two districts, however, Ravana has a very different reputation. His statue presides over temples, and he is worshipped as a god. "[These people] believe that Ravana who was their king was a learned person, well versed with [the important religious texts] and an ardent [religious] devotee,"[4] explains a local politician.

Demons of Japan

No such debate exists where the Oni of Japan are concerned. These demons, which originated in the ancient Shinto belief system, are considered to be bad in every way. Angry and malicious, they delight in bringing illness, injury, insanity, and other troubles to humans. They also love the taste of mortal flesh, and they eat people whenever they get the chance.

The Oni have ugly bodies to match their monstrous personalities. Traditional Japanese artwork depicts the Oni as giant ogreish beings with horns, sharp teeth, hairy faces, and three glaring eyes. They have three fingers on each hand and three toes on each foot. All of these appendages end in wicked claws. Most Oni are green, but these demons may be blue, black, pink, or red as well. They often carry spiked clubs called *kanabo*, which they use to batter anyone or anything that gets in their way.

The Oni may be scary, strong, and dangerous. But luckily for the mortal population, they are not invincible. Brave humans can and often do defeat these demons. These battles are a frequent subject of Japanese folklore.

One popular tale of this type comes from Oe Town, a rural community known for its many Oni-related legends. Village residents swear that long ago, a gang of Oni lived atop nearby Mount Oe. The Oni were vulgar and vicious, and they often visited Oe Town to rob the villagers and steal their daughters. After many years of this ill treatment, a warrior named Minamoto-no-Raiko decided to take 600 soldiers into the mountains and kill the Oni. Minamoto-no-Raiko succeeded, forever ending Oe Town's demon troubles.

The villagers may feel safer these days—but they have not forgotten their past. To this day, townspeople still tell stories about their former Oni neighbors and the troubles they inflicted on the community. They have taken steps to preserve these tales through the Japanese Oni Exchange Museum, a facility dedicated to cataloging the area's unique memories, mementos, and legends. Popular among tourists and historians alike, the museum is helping to keep the demon lore of Japan alive.

Demons of China

Demon lore is also alive and well in China, where spiritual beliefs center around a concept called opposition. This concept states that everything is balanced by an opposite. Thus, light is balanced by dark; male is balanced by female; luck is balanced by misfortune; and good, of course, is balanced by bad. Demons and other evil spirits are therefore an inevitable and, indeed, an essential part of the natural order.

Many Chinese demons get their start as beings called Gui (also spelled Kuei or Kui). Gui are the ghosts of the dead, and they walk freely among the living. They are harmless if they are kept happy through offerings and prayers. If Gui are neglected or dishonored, however, they may become angry. In this case, explains one writer, "[They] may attack human beings to prompt them to meet the ghosts' needs or at least to draw attention to their plight."[5]

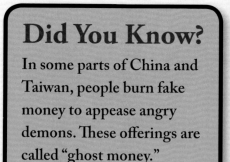

Did You Know?

In some parts of China and Taiwan, people burn fake money to appease angry demons. These offerings are called "ghost money."

Demonic Powers

Demons embody everything people find terrifying. It is not surprising, therefore, that these beings are thought to possess every imaginable supernatural ability. If something is scary or dangerous, demons can do it.

Powers that are commonly attributed to demons include:

- **Mental control.** Many demons can read people's thoughts and communicate via mental telepathy, without the need for spoken words. They can also move objects with mental power alone.
- **Shape-shifting.** Many demons can change their form at will. They can take the shape of mist, plants, animals, or even people.
- **Time manipulation.** Some demons can see the future (although imperfectly). They can sometimes hop from one time period to another.
- **Animal control.** Some demons have a special link with animals, especially those that are poisonous or otherwise unpleasant. They can direct these animals to hurt or terrify human beings.
- **Binding.** Demons can sometimes place curses on humans, and they have the power to make and enforce supernatural contracts.
- **Nature control.** Many demons can control the weather and other natural forces. Especially powerful demons can cause earthquakes, hurricanes, tornadoes, and other natural disasters.

Angry Gui must be appeased right away. If they are not, they become increasingly dangerous and damaging. They may try to harm not only their own living relatives but unrelated people as well. Over time they can even become evil. When this happens, the once-human Gui has transformed itself into a demon.

Some of these demons are well known in Chinese lore. One famous demon, Gonggong, looked like a cross between a human and a snake. After losing a battle with a god, Gonggong tried to kill himself by slamming into one of the sky's supporting pillars. This action caused the sky to rip, unleashing a huge flood and a storm of flames. This disaster, it is said, made the rivers of China flow southeastward into the Pacific Ocean, a situation that persists to the present day.

Less damaging but more common is the Huli Jing, or Fox Fairy. This class of demon roams the Chinese countryside, emerging from graveyards in the dark of night. It can take any shape it likes, but it appears most often as a fox. It loves to trick people into believing the opposite of what is true—that black is white, for example, or that ugly is beautiful. It especially loves to toy with scholars, who are much too rational and reasonable for the Huli Jing's taste. The fox demon is happy if it can confuse or even kill these infuriating mortals.

Islamic Demons

Confusion and death are also the calling cards of the jinn, a class of spirits that causes endless trouble in Islamic tradition. Jinn are thought to be one of the three classes of beings created by Allah (God), along with angels and humans. Like people, jinn have free will and can choose to be good or bad. The jinn themselves explain this situation in a passage from Islam's holy book, the Qur'an: "And among us there are righteous folk and among us there are far from that. We are sects having different rules. . . . And there are some among us who have surrendered (to Allah) and there are among us some who are unjust. . . . And as for those who are unjust, they are firewood for hell."[6]

Demonic jinn fall into several categories. One frightening variety is the Ghul, a shape-shifting monster that lives in desert burial grounds. The Ghul can turn itself into any animal but is most com-

> # Did You Know?
>
> Bats are considered demonic by many African tribespeople. The giant fruit-eating bat of Ghana has a particularly bad reputation. It is said to kidnap travelers and feed them to evil spirits.

Ancient Hindu lore tells of a demon king called Ravana (pictured), a frightening creature with 10 heads and 20 arms. Ravana is still considered a symbol of evil in much of India.

fortable as a hyena. It likes to lure mortal travelers into the desert, then kill and eat them. If no travelers are to be found, the Ghul will approach civilized areas to prey on children and drink their blood. It sometimes even plunders fresh graves and eats the corpses buried within. After performing this gruesome act, the Ghul can assume the form of the body it has just devoured.

Even worse than the Ghul are the Ifrit, a particularly nasty class of jinn. These demons, explain one author, "are not minor disruptive spirits but are exceptionally dangerous, powerful, smart, and malevolent. They don't like people. . . . Many authorities perceive them as lacking any redeeming qualities."[7]

Written on the Skin

A quick peek into any tattoo shop reveals wall upon wall of demonic designs. From scary to cartoonish, foreign to friendly, demons are among the most enduringly popular of all tattoo themes.

Tattoo enthusiasts cite many reasons for this popularity. Some people feel that their souls are dark and tortured. They want tattoos that represent this feeling, and they believe demons are the perfect match. Other people perceive themselves as mischievous, free-spirited, and outside the law. For these people, too, demons may be a good choice.

Some people take a more intellectual approach. They view demon tattoos as a way to preserve their culture's history and beliefs. This type of thinking is common in Japan, where tattoo masters often turn to folklore in general and demon stories in particular for inspiration.

A world-famous tattoo artist named Horiyoshi III is renowned for this type of work. Horiyoshi III is fascinated by Japan's traditional demons and has turned many of them into works of art—on people's skin. The most striking of these designs are collected in a book called *100 Demons of Horiyoshi III*. Hard to find and very expensive, this volume is considered a classic by tattooists and historians alike.

These traits are well illustrated in "The Second Kalandar's Tale," a classic story from an Arabian epic called *The Tales of the Thousand and One Nights*. This story concerns an Ifrit who kidnaps a 12-year-old girl and forces her to become his wife. Twenty-five years later, a traveler discovers the now-adult maiden and falls in love with her. This situation enrages the Ifrit. In a graphic and disturbing passage, the jealous demon brutally tortures his wife in punishment for her transgressions. He then hunts down the suitor. The Ifrit forces the lovesick traveler to watch as he chops off his wife's hands, then her feet, and finally her head.

Demons of Africa

The Ifrit is not the world's only spouse-slaying demon. In the African nation of Angola, a demon called the Kishi plays a similar role. The Kishi is a monstrous, man-eating beast that can disguise itself as a human male. It does this when it wants to enter the mortal world and find a wife.

One Angolan legend tells of a woman who meets and marries a handsome young man. The newlyweds settle into married life in the man's house, which is far from the bride's village. Happy and in love, the young wife is thrilled when she becomes pregnant. Nine months later, however, the woman's joy turns to horror when her baby is born with two heads—one human and one hyena. The woman realizes that her husband is a Kishi, and she knows she is in terrible danger. She flees. But the demon pursues her and soon catches her. Now in its natural form, the beast devours its unlucky wife. Afterward, it returns to raise the demonic child, who turns out to love the taste of human flesh just as much as its daddy does.

The Kishi may be a particularly fearsome specimen. But it is only one among many, many African demons. Each tribe on this continent has its own beliefs concerning the spirit world. Demons and other evil spirits figure prominently in nearly all of these traditions.

A good example comes from the Hausa tribe of West Africa. According to this tribe's belief system, demons cause practically every human malady, with specific demons taking charge of specific problems. The demon Bidda, for instance, causes stiffness. The demon Taiki causes swelling of the stomach. The demon Mahalbiya causes sores and ulcers. The demon Kworrom lives under tree roots and makes travelers trip and stumble. And the demon Sarikin Bakka causes madness in its unlucky human victims.

The everyday demons of the Hausa and other African tribes are still feared and respected in many parts of Africa where tribal lore walks hand in hand with modern belief systems. But these demons are not considered quite as horrifying as the supremely evil beings of many other traditions. They have limited power, and people have ways of dealing with them when the need arises. For this reason, most African demons are seen as unpleasant but unavoidable facts of life, much like bad weather or other natural forces.

Demons of South America

Tribal lore has also played an important role in South America. Like Africa, this continent has been home to countless unique tribes, with each tribe having its own religious beliefs. Demons of all sorts pop up in the legends of these groups.

One interesting legend comes from the Mapuche tribe of south-central Chile and southwestern Argentina. It describes demonic creatures called Wekufe or Huecuve. These beings are born from the forces that tend to disturb or destroy the balance of the universe. They do not have souls, and they are inherently evil. They take great delight in causing earthquakes, insect plagues, and animal diseases. They also love to sicken and kill human beings. Death, unfortunately, does not end this torment. The Wekufe are said to catch and enslave the souls of their victims, forcing them to perform evil acts as eternal demonic assistants.

The Korupira of the Brazilian rainforest also have power over people's souls. Unlike the Wekufe, however, these demons are not considered to be evil. They are actually helpful beings that protect animals and heal them when they are sick or wounded. They usually leave humans alone—but they become enraged when hunters hurt animals needlessly, kill for fun, or are wasteful in any other way. When a person does any of these things, a Korupira inflicts various punishments. It may simply taunt someone who commits a minor transgression. For more serious offenses, a Korupira may make a hunter stumble or cause him to become lost in the deep woods.

Only in the worst cases will a Korupira inflict the ultimate penalty: the theft of the hunter's soul and, subsequently, his death.

The Korupira and the Wekufe have very different habits and personalities, but both have something to do with the balance of nature. The Wekufe disrupt the balance; the Korupira try to maintain it. Either way, humans wind up as the victims. It just goes to show that helpful or harmful, any demon can cause a problem for the unlucky mortals it encounters.

Demons of North America

The native tribes of North America were well aware of this fact. According to the legends of these tribes, demons can and often do intrude on the human world. These demons run the gamut from mildly irritating to dangerous and even, sometimes, deadly.

The traditional demons of the Inuit people are a particularly nasty group. Known collectively as the Tunerak, these beings are

Two Oni, one taking a bath and the other assisting, are depicted in this nineteenth-century Japanese painting. These ogreish demons of Japanese lore often have horns, sharp teeth, hairy faces, and three eyes. They also come in many colors including green and red.

vicious, relentless, and hungry for human flesh. Death is the almost inevitable result when mortals encounter these creatures.

One Inuit legend concerns a demon called the Wi-lu-gho-yuk. This being is small and furry, much like a mouse. It lurks in icy ponds. When a human passes above, the Wi-lu-gho-yuk passes magically through the ice and gnaws its way into the person's foot. It burrows upward through flesh and bone until it reaches the heart, which it devours. The Wi-lu-gho-yuk then bursts out of the chest and returns to the pond to await its next victim.

Demons known simply as Water Babies are also said to inhabit watery areas. Originating with the Washo tribespeople of California, these creatures look like gray-skinned human infants with stubby arms and legs. They mew like kittens to lure humans into lakes, then work in groups to submerge and drown their victims.

Killing people is bad enough. But when the need arises, the Water Babies can do much worse. They are said, for example, to have caused the devastating San Francisco earthquake of 1906. One Washo tribe member tells the story this way:

> There was this white man up here fishing. He caught a Water Baby but he didn't know what it was. He thought it was some kind of fish and took it to San Francisco and they put it that place where they have a lotta fish [aquarium]. [A Washo official] went all the way down there to tell the mayor that they had better let that Water Baby loose, but nobody would pay no attention to him. Well you know they had a big earthquake down there and the water came up around everything. When it was all over that tank where they had the Water Baby was empty.[8]

Demons Everywhere

The Water Baby tale and other stories from the Americas, from Africa, and Asia are undeniably dramatic. But they are far from unique. Every culture and religion has demons that cause natural disasters, personal misfortunes, and all other varieties of evil.

Caribbean tradition offers one good example. In this culture, demonic beings called Duppies or Jumbies cause constant trouble. These creatures can possess humans or, sometimes, eat them. Some scholars consider Duppies to be ghosts. As folklorist Andrew Munroe points out, however, "[The words] duppy and jumbie have gone into use as any of a number of supernatural elements, many of which seem to have an irregular connection to having once been living, if at all, and so maybe [they are] more demons or other inhabitants of the supernatural realm than lost or wandering souls."[9]

The Hantu of the Philippines also have a mixture of ghostly and demonic qualities. Some Hantu are clearly the angry souls of dead humans. Others are true otherworldly beings that have never been mortal and that bring all sorts of problems into the human realm. One example is Hantu Raya, an evil entity that sometimes forms pacts with people. Hantu Raya helps its mortal owners in return for regular offerings. If the offerings cease, the owners face horribly painful deaths and eternal enslavement as Hantu Raya's minions.

The list goes on and on. The Aborigines of Australia and the Maori of New Zealand recognize entire pantheons of demons. So do or did the ancient Scandinavians, the Slavs, the Icelanders, the peoples of the Pacific Islands, and groups from every other imaginable culture. The demons of these traditions are very different in looks, personalities, and functions, but they all have something in common: They cause bad things. From petty annoyances to major disasters, every mortal problem can be and probably has been blamed on meddlesome demons.

Chapter 2

Demons in Charge

Over the ages, an astonishing number of demons have been identified by various belief systems. Jewish tradition, for example, states that precisely 7,405,926 demons are in existence—no more, no less. The Christian hell, according to some scholars, contains more than 130 million demons. And as recently as the early 1900s, residents of Korea were said by one source to "number their demons by thousands of billions; they fill the chimney, the shed, the living-room, the kitchen, they are on every shelf and jar; in thousands they waylay the traveller as he leaves his home, beside him, behind him, dancing in front of him, whirring, over his head, crying out upon him from air, earth and water."[10]

With so much competition, for a single demon to attract much attention seems almost impossible. But it turns out that in demon society, as in the mortal world, someone usually comes out on top. "Boss" demons are immeasurably more evil, powerful, and meddlesome than the everyday demons over which they rule. They inspire a deeper, more elemental fear as a result. Bad to the bone, these beings are truly the stuff of humankind's worst nightmares.

Mara, the Tempter

In Buddhist tradition, desire is the root of all human unhappiness. People crave all sorts of things: wealth, power, love, possessions, experiences, and even basic needs like food and drink. The devout Buddhist seeks to vanquish these desires and all others through meditation and prayer. A blissful state called Nirvana, or enlightenment, awaits the man or woman who succeeds in this quest.

Reaching Nirvana, unfortunately, is almost impossible thanks to a demon called Mara. The Buddhists consider Mara to be the personification of evil as well as the lord of misfortune, sin, destruction, and death. He does not want anyone to reach enlightenment. He therefore spends a great deal of time tempting people away from the path of righteousness. As one author says, "Mara reviles man, blinds him, guides him toward sensuous desires; once man is in his bondage, Mara is free to destroy him."[11]

Mara famously tried to sway a holy man named Prince Siddhartha in this way. Legend says that Mara came to Siddhartha during a meditation session. First the demon appealed to Siddhartha's sense of duty, begging him not to abandon his responsibilities as a father, husband, and ruler. But the prince was unmoved. Next, Mara tried to frighten Siddhartha by threatening to shoot him with a bow and arrow. This tactic failed as well. Finally, Mara summoned a legion of demons to beset and distract the meditating prince. Siddhartha ignored them all. He reached Nirvana in the midst of the chaos to earn the title of Buddha, which means "Enlightened One."

This story proves that Mara is not invincible. Indeed, Buddhist tradition states that thousands of people have conquered the demon's temptations and reached Nirvana. This number is tiny, however, compared to the vast number of people who have sought enlightenment since Buddhism was introduced about 2,500 years ago. It is clear that Mara's lies and temptations have been incredibly effective through the ages—and they are still working today. As author and scholar Jnana Sipe puts it, "Mara's army is just as real to us today as it was to the Buddha. . . . The tempestuous longings and fears that assail us, as well as the views and opinions that confine us, are sufficient evidence of . . . our current cohabitation with the devil."[12]

Evil God of the Aztecs

The demon Mara concerns himself mostly with living people. The head demon of Aztec tradition, by contrast, is much more concerned with the dead. Known as Mictlantecuhtli (meekt-lahn-te-KOOT-ly), this evil entity is the god of death. He is also the ruler of Mictlan, the Aztec underworld, which has been described as "a fearsome place of torments and pestilence, where one drinks pus and eats scabs."[13] In Mictlan the souls of the dead live in squalor as weasels, stink beetles, and other unpleasant creatures.

The lord of this realm, not surprisingly, is a terrible sight to behold. Mictlantecuhtli is usually depicted as a blood-spattered skeleton or, sometimes, as a person with a toothy skull for a head. The skull's ear holes are often plugged with human bones. A necklace of eyeballs hangs around Mictlantecuhtli's scrawny neck. In his hand the demon god holds an ax or a dagger, which he uses to remove mortals' hearts. After performing this gruesome deed, Mictlantecuhtli devours the still-twitching organ to satisfy his never-ending bloodlust.

This bloodlust was a constant concern for the Aztec people. The Aztecs believed that Mictlantecuhtli would become angry and vengeful if he was allowed to become hungry. He would then mistreat the poor souls of Mictlan, which of course were the dead relatives of those still living. To prevent this from happening, Aztec priests made regular human sacrifices to Mictlantecuhtli. Sometimes they even engaged in ritual cannibalism themselves. They hoped that these activities would please their demon god and put him in a good mood.

Offerings of weapons, pots, and other desirable goods were considered another way to placate Mictlantecuhtli. The best way to deliver these offerings, it was thought, was to bury them with the

The ancient Aztec god of death, Mictlantecuhtli (pictured), rules the underworld. This demon's thirst for human blood is said to be infinite.

dead. Departed souls carried the items with them to the underworld. Upon arrival in Mictlan, they gave the items to Mictlantecuhtli in the hope of winning the god's favor and avoiding any torments the capricious demon might choose to inflict.

Worship of Mictlantecuhtli and other Aztec deities peaked in the late 1400s and early 1500s. After this period, the Aztec Empire collapsed, and its gods and demons slowly slid from prominence. To most people today they are just an interesting and bloody historical footnote. In a few places, however, Mictlan and its demonic ruler are still very much remembered—and feared. To this day, people in some parts of Mexico still worry that caves may be portals to Mictlantecuhtli's realm. These people, says one historian, "still seal up caves with bags because from them emanate vapors full of disease, death, and the smell of decay."[14]

The Essence of Evil

Mictlantecuhtli was one of the bloodiest demons ever to appear in any belief system. But despite his disturbing taste for human flesh, the Aztec god of death was not considered totally evil. Mictlantecuhtli actually had some very positive qualities, including the power to create life when he so chose. He thus had the ability to do good or, at the very least, to refrain from doing harm.

The top demon of Zoroastrianism, a belief system that originated and peaked in ancient Persia, has no such redeeming traits. The wicked Ahriman, also called Angra Mainyu, is thought to be the essence of evil. This demon delights in creating anger, greed, envy, lust, and every other harmful or negative emotion known to mankind. He also brings chaos, death, disease, and other ills into the mortal realm. When he is not visiting misfortunes upon the living, Ahriman turns his attention to the dead. This demon rules a realm that is very similar to Christianity's hell. His subjects are the souls of people who have lived sinful lives. Ahriman collects these souls immediately after death, when they are forced to pass over an "accountant's bridge." Each soul is judged during this passage. Pious souls are permitted to pass. Those judged unworthy are pulled into

The Names of Satan

The King James Version of the Bible refers to Satan by many different names. Titles for the devil include Abaddon; the Accuser; the Adversary; the Angel of Light; the Antichrist; Apollyon; the Beast; Beelzebub; the Deceiver; the Dragon; the Enemy; the Evil One; the Father of Lies; the King of the Bottomless Pit; Leviathan; the Liar; Roaring Lion; the Serpent; the Tempter; and the Wicked One.

Over the ages, Satan has also earned many familiar nicknames that do not appear in the Bible. The demon is often called the Prince of Lies because of his deceptive ways. Less formally, he is sometimes called Old Scratch, Old Gooseberry, Pocker, Mr. Sam, or Old Nick. In France, he may be called Le Cornu, which means "the horned one." This name is a reference to the goat's horns that protrude from the devil's awful skull.

the void, where they suffer eternal punishment at Ahriman's merciless hands.

Ahriman certainly enjoys this cruel job. The demon's ultimate goal, however, has nothing to do with humankind. Ahriman's primary purpose is to oppose another Zoroastrian deity named Ahura Mazda, who is the essence of good. Ahriman envies and detests this sublime being. Everything the demon god does is designed to torment and, he hopes, eventually overcome his otherworldly rival.

Luckily for Ahura Mazda, Ahriman is not very bright. He constantly foils his own evil efforts. In one legend, Ahriman creates a frog and tells it to drink the world's entire water supply. The frog performs this task flawlessly. But moments later a housefly—also one of Ahriman's creations—crawls into the frog's nose. The frog vomits the water, thus reversing the terrible drought Ahriman had worked so hard to cause.

Lord of the Jinni

Ahriman may have limitations, but he never stops trying to create problems in both the divine and human realms. The same is true of Iblis, the primary demon of Islam. Iblis is also sometimes called Shaitan or Shaytan, an Arabic word that has been translated as "adversarial," "opposing," or "evil." All of these translations boil down to the same thing: Iblis is God's eternal opponent and the enemy of humankind. He is, simply stated, the devil.

The Qur'an states that Allah created Iblis. He began his existence as a jinni like any other. The young demon soon rose in status, however, because he was exceptionally devoted to his creator. He kept company with Allah's angels and was considered the holiest of the jinn.

But deep in his heart, Iblis was secretly prideful. He hid this sinful attitude from Allah for a long time. His true feelings became clear only when Allah ordered all of his heavenly creations to bow to Adam, the first human man. All of the angels obeyed Allah's command—but Iblis refused. "I am better than him. Thou createdst me of fire while him Thou didst create of mud,"[15] he complained. This disobedience infuriated Allah, who cast the once-favored Iblis out of heaven forever.

Iblis was mortified by this turn of events. Angry and rejected, the demon hardened his heart against Allah and vowed to tempt humankind away from the path of righteousness. He assumed leadership of the jinn and directed his minions to whisper evil into the hearts of mortals everywhere. This whispering, says Islam, continues to the present day and is the source of every sinful human urge. People who obey these urges become followers of Iblis and are degraded in the eyes of Allah, just like their demonic master.

Iblis's temptations may be potent. Luckily for the Muslim population, however, they are also limited. Iblis cannot actually harm peo-

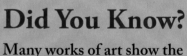

Did You Know?

Many works of art show the demon god Mara's temptation of the Buddha. Mara is often pictured riding an elephant or holding lightning bolts in his hands.

ple; he can only try to sway them. Furthermore, the demon king is forbidden by Allah to bother truly devout individuals. A pure heart, therefore, is the only defense a person needs to repel this evil yet divinely constrained entity.

Asmodeus, Demon of Lust

Scholars note that the top demons of Zoroastrianism and Islam both emerged around the same time, between the years 500 and 600. The cultures that spawned these demons had plenty of contact. It is no surprise, therefore, that their top monsters developed some striking similarities. These demons influenced other belief systems, too—particularly Judaism. Established centuries before the birth of Christ, Judaism originally had very little to do with demons. But Ahriman and Iblis had a deep impact on Jewish thought. Before

A manuscript page from the ancient world depicts the Aztecs conducting rituals of human sacrifice. Hoping to please the demon god, Aztec priests made frequent sacrifices to Mictlantecuhtli.

long, Judaism had its own demon king: the altogether unpleasant Asmodeus.

Asmodeus is a frightful entity with clawed cock's feet and three heads—one of a bull, one of a ram, and one of a man. He has many dread duties, including running hell's gambling houses and sowing discontent among the human population. His most important job, though, is using lust as a tool to destroy mortal relationships, especially marriages. The demon explains his work in this passage:

> My business is to plot against the newly wedded, so that they may not know one another. And I sever them utterly by many calamities; and I waste away the beauty of virgins and estrange their hearts . . . I transport men into fits of madness and desire when they have wives of their own, so that they leave them and go off by night and day to others that belong to other men; with the result that they commit sin and fall into murderous deeds.[16]

One of Asmodeus's most gruesome moments is described in a work called the *Book of Tobias*. Asmodeus is smitten with a virginal woman named Sara. When Sara weds, the jealous demon slays the bridegroom before the wedding night can arrive. Sara, still a virgin, eventually remarries—but the second husband dies at Asmodeus's hands as well. This process repeats itself five more times, with the unlucky Sara remaining pure throughout. The cycle is finally broken when Sara marries Tobias, her eighth husband. The archangel Raphael takes pity on the human couple and banishes Asmodeus before he can thwart Sara's happiness yet again.

This story highlights an interesting aspect of Asmodeus's role. It is clear that the demon king is malicious and powerful, and he has the ability to do great harm. At the same time, however, he is firmly under divine control. He can and will be stopped if God finds his activities tiresome. So while Asmodeus may be the top demon, the Jewish people have never considered him a serious threat.

Satan, the Worst Demon of All

The head demon of the Christian pantheon is a different matter entirely. Known as Satan or simply the devil, this being is pure evil and a constant threat to humankind. He is similar to Asmodeus in that he must bow to God's authority when commanded. But the Christian God very seldom interferes in Satan's grim activities. God gives his adversary almost unlimited freedom to carry out his unholy work.

Dishonorable Mentions

Over the ages, only a few demons have earned top billing in their respective belief systems. But many other demons are deeply feared in certain circles. The following demons earn special dishonorable mentions for their nasty reputations or lasting influence:

Supay. In Incan mythology, this demon was the god of death and the ruler of the underworld. Today, traditional South American dances called diabladas still pay tribute to this demon god.

Lilith. In Jewish tradition, Lilith was Adam's first wife. Lilith eventually abandoned Adam and became a demon. In this role, she caused infertility in both men and women and killed human infants.

Vritra. According to Hindu belief, Vritra was the head of the demonic Asana tribe. Usually depicted as a serpent or a dragon, he brought drought and misfortune to people everywhere.

Baphomet. This pagan demon has a goat's head, horns, and lower body; eaglelike wings; and a human torso. Baphomet is best known for his fearsome appearance, which is the basis for many classic demonic images.

The Christian devil, known as Satan, runs hell as a place of eternal torture and torment—a vision captured in this fifteenth-century painting by Giovanni da Modena. Satan's arsenal for seducing humans includes lies, bargains, and temptation.

The scope of this work is unparalleled in demonology. In popular Christian thinking, Satan is ultimately responsible for every bad thing that ever happens anywhere, to anyone. His duties include running the Christian hell, which is a place of eternal torture and torment; overseeing millions upon millions of demonic subordinates; causing natural disasters; creating and spreading filth and disease; and consorting with sorcerers and witches. Most important in people's everyday lives, however, is Satan's never-ending quest to seduce humans away from God. Through lies, bargains, and temptations, the devil turns weak mortals into his infernal pawns.

In this respect, Satan's greatest triumph may have occurred in the Garden of Eden mere moments after God created humankind. According to the book of Genesis in the Christian Bible, Satan came to the first woman, Eve, disguised as a serpent. He tempted her to eat fruit from a forbidden tree. Eve surrendered to the serpent's urging and convinced Adam, the first man, to do the same. It seemed like a small matter—until God discovered the pair's transgression. Furious with Adam and Eve's disobedience, God heaped a series of eternal misfortunes upon humankind. He then banished the first man and woman from the Garden of Eden, leaving them forever vulnerable to Satan's enticements.

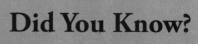

Did You Know?

The Qur'an states that Iblis is allowed to tempt humankind only until the Day of Judgment arrives. After that day, the demon king will be thrown into hell for all eternity.

Satan's Origin and Evolution

The Adam and Eve tale is Satan's first biblical appearance. The demon's story, however, begins long before this point. The Bible explains that Satan was once a high-ranking angel among God's heav-

enly host. His name at this time may have been Lucifer, although scholars disagree on this point.

Scholars do agree that much like Iblis, Satan/Lucifer started to think too highly of himself. He became so proud that he thought he was better than God himself. "I will ascend into heaven, I will exalt my throne above the stars of God. . . . I will ascend above the heights of the clouds; I will be like the most High,"[17] he boasts in one biblical passage.

This pride quickly leads to Satan's downfall. God becomes angry with Satan's inappropriate attitude. He appoints the archangel Michael to lead an army of angels against Satan and his followers. A battle ensues, with Michael defeating Satan. As the Bible states: "And the great dragon was cast out, that old serpent, called the Devil, and Satan, which deceiveth the whole world: he was cast out into the earth, and his angels were cast out with him."[18]

The Bible is not clear on what happens next. Some scholars think that Satan tumbled all the way to hell. Others believe that he fell into the mortal sphere, where he roams invisibly and relentlessly to this day. "The belief that Satan is in Hell is a product of cartoons and movies. . . . Satan is not in Hell and probably spends most of his time on earth, seeking to destroy the lives of human beings and to keep them separated from God,"[19] states one fundamentalist Christian Web site.

The Devil Wears Many Disguises

To do this job, Satan has to earn people's trust. This means that he must avoid scaring them away. This is no easy feat for a creature as fearsome as the devil. In classic works of art, Satan usually appears huge and muscular, with beet-red skin. His legs are often goatlike, ending in cloven hooves. The demon's eyes are wicked and glowing, and his broad forehead bears two sharp horns. A long, barbed tail protrudes from the base of Satan's spine, and two batlike wings sprout between his mighty shoulder blades. As a whole, the demon's look is more likely to inspire horror than confidence.

Satan dodges this problem by transforming himself when he interacts with mortals. The devil is a master of disguise, with the ability to look like anything he chooses—an animal, an inanimate object, a flame, or even a human being. He maintains the chosen form until a human is firmly in his power. Only then, when it is too late for the victim to flee, does the demon show his true form or otherwise reveal himself.

A folktale from the American Southwest offers a classic example of this concept. As the story goes, a young woman attends a local

> **Did You Know?**
>
> According to Jewish legend, the demon king Asmodeus is half human. His mother was a mortal and his father was a fallen angel.

dance, where she meets a handsome stranger with jet-black hair and clothes. Not realizing that the stranger is really the devil, the woman enthusiastically agrees to a dance. This agreement places the woman in the devil's power. On the dance floor, the demon twirls his dance partner so long and hard that her feet become hot. The floor melts away, and then the girl melts as well. Afterward, says the tale, "The man in black bowed once to the crowd and disappeared. The Devil had come to his party and he had spun the girl all the way to hell."[20]

Another tale tells of a priest who finds a mysterious horse tied outside his home one morning. The horse "was a magnificent animal, pitch black in color, tall, sleek and rippling with muscle. It had a wicked gleam in its black eyes. . . . The priest realized at once that this horse was . . . the Devil himself!"[21] Still, the priest needs a horse, so he names the evil beast "Old Nick" and puts it to work. All is well, until one day a man unbuckles the horse's bridle so the animal can take a drink. Old Nick takes off like lightning. It leaps onto a large river rock, which instantly cracks apart to reveal a deep cavern. The horse flees into the cavern, never to be seen again. But the hole remains to this day as a reminder of the community's brush with the devil.

Everyday Evil

Stories like these make an important point about Christianity's top demon. They show that he can be anywhere and anything. People must therefore be constantly alert for signs of the devil at work.

Other cultures might not focus quite so much on actual demonic appearances. But they do worry about the effects of top demons on their everyday lives. The temptations of Mara, the hunger of Mictlantecuhtli, the whispers of Iblis, and other demonic disruptions have threatened mortal health and happiness for thousands of years—and this wicked work shows no sign of stopping. Powerful and evil, humankind's top demons are sure to inspire new nightmares for untold generations of people yet to come.

Chapter 3

Associating with Demons

Many people swear that demons do not exist. They think that these beings are just legends—ways to explain things that go wrong. They do not believe that a real demon would or, indeed, could appear to terrorize a real person.

Other people, however, feel very differently. They are absolutely convinced that demons exist and that they interact with humans on a regular basis. Some of these interactions are accidental. Some occur when demons stalk unwitting mortal victims. And still others happen when people summon or otherwise consort with the powers of darkness. Whatever the cause, contact does happen—in superstition, tradition, and religion, where demonic encounters appear as an accepted fact of human life.

Where Demons Lurk

Most demonic encounters happen, not surprisingly, in places where demons are known to lurk. Different traditions identify many types of demon homes and haunts.

Geographic locations are one such haunt. Some demons are said to live in certain areas or spots. The Kappa of Japan, for example, are vampire demons with basin-shaped heads. The demons must keep these basins full of water to avoid losing their magical powers. They therefore stay in or near water at all times.

The Patupaiarehe of New Zealand's Maori people are also tied to a specific place. These demons are said to inhabit deserted graveyards, far from human settlements. The Patupaiarehe long for human flesh—and because they rarely see people, they are always starving. They will viciously attack and eat any person who wanders too close. To avoid these horrible creatures, the Maori play it safe and stay away from all graveyards, just in case.

Demon Thresholds

In many cultures the same is true of thresholds, places where one element meets another. These border areas are sometimes physical. The forest's edge, for example, is the place where fields meet woods, and

The Kappa of Japanese lore (pictured) are vampirelike demons whose magical powers depend on water. Legends say that as long as their basin-shaped heads are filled with water, the demons hold great powers.

藤枝

能善寺

蓮華寺

の自刻像

人

the seashore is the place where the land meets the ocean. Thresholds can also be spiritual. A graveyard, for example, is the place where life meets death. These areas and many others are considered meeting points between the human and spirit worlds. They are therefore notorious for harboring demons and other evil entities.

Most humans cross one threshold every day: the one that leads into and out of their homes. Some cultures believe that demons are especially likely to gather near these places. "That's the root reason behind the common superstition urging people to step over, not on, a threshold. No need to wake or annoy any resident spirits,"[22] explains author and spiritualist Judika Illes.

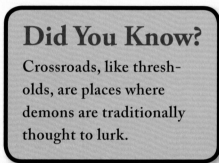

Did You Know?

Crossroads, like thresholds, are places where demons are traditionally thought to lurk.

This superstition gave rise to a wedding ritual that is commonly practiced to this day. Tradition dictates that a bridegroom must carry the bride into the couple's new home. This tradition is fun, romantic, and usually accompanied by squeals of delight. Most newlyweds do not realize that it is also deadly serious. As Illes explains, "Universal folklore considers brides especially vulnerable to jealous spirits. The tradition of carrying the bride over the threshold emerged as a safety precaution."[23] By leaping over the threshold, newlyweds are actually trying to avoid unwanted demonic attention.

Unwanted Attention

This type of attention, unfortunately, is all too easy to attract. Demons are said to be very interested in the mortal world, and they are always on the lookout for human targets. They are irresistibly drawn to people who seem vulnerable to demonic influence.

An unusual interest in demons may be one such sign of vulnerability. An example would be teenagers who listen to music with demonic lyrics, wear infernal jewelry, and get demon tattoos on their skin. According to certain belief systems, these young men and women are laying out the welcome mat for evil entities—and demons are almost certain to respond to the invitation. When they do, they inflict bad luck, depression, addiction, insanity, and other unpleasant consequences upon their unsuspecting victims.

A young man named Mark recounts an experience like this. "My friends and I used to fool around with the occult. We lit candles in graveyards to try and summon ghosts, said the Lord's Prayer backwards at midnight in front of a mirror, prayed to the Devil on Halloween. We just thought it was a bit of fun, we didn't ever believe in any of it,"[24] he remembers.

One night, however, Mark says a demon started to communicate with him. At first the entity was nice. It became more and more ornery over time, however, until Mark finally told the demon to leave

A Deal with the Devil

Christian tradition states that mortals can make pacts with the devil or other demons. In these pacts, people ask a demon for wealth, knowledge, power, or other earthly favors. The demon gets eternal control over the person's soul in return.

A famous German legend about a scholar named Faust describes one such bargain. In this tale, Faust begs the devil for unlimited knowledge and worldly pleasures. The devil agrees to the deal and sends a demonic representative, Mephistopheles, to act as Faust's servant. Mephistopheles remains at Faust's side for many years, fulfilling his every selfish wish. The scholar enjoys himself tremendously until the end of the agreed-upon period, when his soul is dragged forever into hell.

Faust manages to avoid this fate in Johann Wolfgang von Goethe's play *Faust*, which is probably the best-known version of the Faust tale. In Goethe's work, the scholar uses Mephistopheles' gifts to do good. His soul is eventually rescued by a band of angels, who recognize the value of Faust's earthly strivings.

and never come back. Later that night, says Mark, "[The demon] clawed at me and bit me. I woke up shredded and bruised."[25] The attacks continued until Mark performed a ceremony to banish his unwelcome visitor.

Seeking Contact

Dabbling in fortune-telling may be another way to draw demonic attention. People who practice tarot, palmistry, astrology, and other mystical arts are seeking contact with the nonhuman realm. Sometimes, it is said, they make contact of a more sinister and even demonic variety.

One woman who claims to have psychic abilities remembers the day she had an encounter of this type. She was performing a ceremony to remove negative energy from an office building. As she worked, she says, "I heard this . . . I don't even know how to rightly describe it. It was a deep voice, and it came to me like it was coming from down a long, very deep tunnel—almost like I shouldn't be

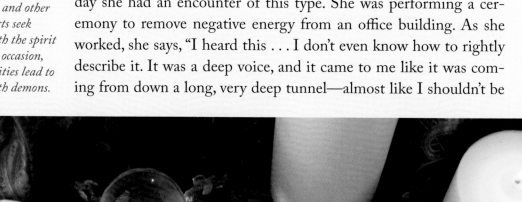

Those who dabble in fortune-telling, the reading of tarot cards (pictured), and other mystical arts seek contact with the spirit world. On occasion, these activities lead to contact with demons.

hearing it. . . . This voice had been so evil that I had gotten cold chills down my spine."[26] To this day, the woman is convinced that the mysterious voice belonged to a demonic visitor.

Some psychics may experience a subtler form of demonic contact. Fortune-tellers and other mystics are seeking information that, some say, humans are not meant to know. Demons cannot resist the temptation to provide this information. At first, a demon may give straight answers. Once the demon earns the psychic's trust, however, it starts to twist the truth. Soon the demon is lying freely to its human contact. The psychic repeats these lies to his or her clients, thus spreading the demon's influence further and further with each passing day.

Portals to Another Dimension

Experienced psychics and mediums are on the lookout for this kind of interference. They tend to be very cautious when they seek contact with the spirit world. Regular folks, however, are not always so careful. Untrained, unbelieving people dabble in the occult all the time. They think they are playing games. These games, though, may have unintended consequences of the demonic variety.

A device called a Ouija board is particularly well known for inviting the attention of demons. This item, which is sold in toy stores as a game, is just a board printed with letters, numbers, and the words YES, NO, and GOOD BYE. Players set an item called a planchette on the board and place their fingers on the planchette. They hope that otherworldly forces will nudge the planchette across the board to spell out various messages.

If all goes well, the planchette moves. Players might be pushing the device themselves—or perhaps, just perhaps, they are actually speaking with benevolent spirits or dead relatives. They ask a few questions and get a few nonsensical answers. The game is fascinating, a little bit creepy, and altogether harmless.

Occasionally, however, players make contact with beings that seem demonic. Stories of these encounters pop up with astonishing regularity. On one Web site, a frequent Ouija user explains how he was stalked by a certain demon:

> One particular spirit always seemed compelled to make its presence known. . . . Too many times to count, it has at first pretended to be a nice spirit, or pretend to be whomever I was trying to contact. But eventually it showed its true self, cussing me, threatening me and others present in the room. Once it actually cussed me using what looked like Latin or Hebrew, and using biblical terminology. I was genuinely fascinated and startled by how many times [this demon] showed up, even in many different states and many different Ouija boards.[27]

This story and others like it come as no surprise to people who believe in demons. It is extremely unwise, these people say, to fool around with Ouija boards or, indeed, with any device that allows contact with evil beings. As one person puts it, "You have no control over who decides to speak to you through [a Ouija board]. The board can open a portal to another dimension, and allow access to this realm. Things come through. Those things can be incredibly difficult to send back."[28]

Ghosts in the Machine

Thanks partly to backlash like this, Ouija boards are not as popular as they were a few decades ago. Many people find the whole concept a bit creepy. They do not truly believe that a Ouija board will attract demons—but they do not quite disbelieve it, either. They keep these devices out of their homes, just in case.

In today's world, unfortunately, this precaution may be pointless. Some demonologists believe that modern homes already contain countless portals to the demon world. To humans, these portals look like harmless bits of technology: television sets, MP3 players, radios, gaming systems. To demons, however, these things are like doorways. They provide easy, always-on access to the mortal plane.

Paralyzed by Fear

A person's mind can actually wake up while the body remains asleep. This condition is called sleep paralysis, and most people experience it at least once or twice in their lifetimes. During an episode of sleep paralysis, people cannot move their bodies. They may have trouble breathing, and they may feel a heavy weight on the chest. These sensations persist until their bodies also become fully awake.

Today, sleep paralysis is considered a medical condition. Traditionally, however, many cultures have believed that this frightening feeling is the work of night-roaming demons. The most common form of this belief states that a demon sits on a sleeper's chest. The demon's weight accounts for the heaviness the sleeper experiences.

In Old English, sleep demons were known as *mare* or *maere*. A visit from one of these demons was thus a nightmare. This word has lost its link to sleep paralysis. But it endures today as a description of the fearful visions that trouble people during their sleep.

Of all technological portals, computers—and especially Internet-connected computers—are considered the worst. These devices can feed pornography, violence, hatred, and other destructive influences to anyone, anywhere, at any time. It seems that they have an almost demonic ability to tempt people into improper thoughts and activities. This ability, say some people, is no coincidence. These people believe that computers do not simply seem to be demonic. They actually are demonic. Somewhere within their cords, wires, and hard drives, they house evil entities that constantly nudge human users toward inappropriate actions.

A religious leader named Jim Peasboro claims that he has encountered one of these entities. He says that when he had an opportunity to examine a supposedly infected computer, an artificial-intelligence program opened automatically. Then, Peasboro says, "The program began talking directly to me, openly mocked me. It typed out, 'Preacher, you are a weakling and your God is a damn liar.' Then the device went haywire and started printing out what looked like gobbledygook. . . . I later had an expert in dead languages examine the text. It turned out to be a stream of obscenities written in a 2,800-year-old Mesopotamian dialect!"[29]

Usually viewed as a fun but harmless game, the Ouija board (pictured) has resulted, some say, in encounters with demons. Such encounters are difficult to confirm.

Based on this experience and others, Peasboro is convinced that demons regularly contact people through computers. He cites examples such as the 1999 shooting massacre in Columbine, Colorado, to support this claim. He points out that the young men who performed the shootings were computer buffs. "I have no doubt that computer demons exerted an influence on them,"[30] he explains.

Associating with Demons

No one will ever know for sure whether Peasboro's claims are valid. But true or false, his ideas sum up some common assumptions: Demons are evil and deceptive. They wish bad things upon people. Interacting with them is dangerous, and sometimes it leads to disastrous consequences. Despite this danger, however, someone is always willing to take the risk. In every culture and every age, people have tried their best to make contact with demons.

Tribal holy men and women, also called shamans, are the primary members of this group. Shamans do not speak with demons because they want to. They do it because it is part of their job and because it is important to the safety of their communities. A shaman seeks out demons only when they become angry and start to torment the human population. He or she does this by using song, dance, prayer, fasting, drugs, or other methods to enter an altered mental state. In this state the shaman finds and speaks with the upset entity, then takes steps to calm it down. A simple animal sacrifice or another offering usually persuades an angry demon to stop meddling in mortal affairs.

Witches are another group historically associated with demons. Belief in witchcraft peaked between the 1500s and 1600s. During this period, many women were accused of being witches and associating with demons. Some supposed witches were even executed for their crimes. Today, historians agree that most of these accusations were baseless. Some of them, however, may have contained a grain of truth. History shows that people have always sought contact with demons. Whether they succeeded or not, some accused witches had undoubtedly engaged in this type of activity.

The *Grimoires*

They were not the only ones to do so. During the same period as the great witch hunts, many people were trying to raise evil entities.

> ### Did You Know?
> Toy manufacturer Parker Brothers has sold more than 10 million Ouija boards since 1967, when the company began producing the device.

Most of these people depended on magical instruction books called *grimoires* to guide their demon-raising sessions.

One well-known *grimoire* is called *The Grand Grimoire*, sometimes called *The Red Dragon*. This book was published sometime between the early 1500s and the 1700s (historians are not sure exactly when). It describes many frightful demons, including their names, habits, and powers. It further explains how to contact each one of these demons and how to enter into pacts with them once they appear. To strike a deal with the demon Lucifuge, for example, the reader is instructed to recite the following passage: "Emperor Lucifer, master of all the rebel spirits, I ask you to be favorable in my summons of your great minister Lucifuge Rofocale, since I wish to make a pact with him. . . . Be propitious & ensure that the great Lucifuge appears to me tonight in human guise & without emitting foul odors & that he grant me as per the pact I will present to him, all of the riches which I require."[31]

A *grimoire* called the *Pseudomonarchia Daemonum* offers similar help. Published around 1583, this book lists 68 demons. It explains the rituals that summon each entity, and also pinpoints the best hours to perform these rituals.

The *Pseudomonarchia* was soon followed by a book called the *Lesser Key of Solomon* or *Lemegeton Clavicula Salomonis*. Published sometime in the 1600s, this *grimoire* mostly copies the demonic list of the *Pseudomonarchia* but adds detailed descriptions of each entity. It also includes expanded information about ritual preparations, magical implements, and other key matters. Most important, perhaps, it contains images of each demon's sigil—an image that captures the essence of the demon. Used properly, these sigils supposedly allow humans to call and subdue the underworld's most powerful beings.

The *Lesser Key of Solomon* and other *grimoires* are anything but sophisticated. Their language is stilted, and their illustrations are

> ## Did You Know?
>
> The demons listed in the *Lesser Key of Solomon*, a book from the 1600s, are known as the Goetic demons. Even today, they are the most called-upon entities in demonic rituals.

shoddy. They seem quaint and old-fashioned, more like antiques than books with any contemporary value. In certain circles, however, these publications are just as important today as ever. Would-be demon worshippers still turn to the *grimoires* for ideas and instructions. Using the books' words and images, they try to pull demons into the human realm.

Enslaving Demons

They have a compelling reason for doing so. Demons may be dangerous, but they are also powerful—and they can use their power to give people practically anything they want. They have unlimited access to money, knowledge, influence, sex, and other things that humans may desperately desire.

The trick, of course, is getting a demon to provide these things. The typical demon is more interested in hurting humans than helping them. If the demon can be enslaved, however, it has no choice but to cooperate. Control is therefore a key goal of those who associate with demons.

The experience of a biblical character named King Solomon shows just how rewarding this control can be. A text called *The Testament of Solomon* explains how the king used a magical ring to enslave dozens of demons and put them to work building a temple: "Some of these demons I condemned to do the heavy work of the construction of the Temple of God. Others I shut up in prisons. Others I ordered to wrestle with fire in (the making of) gold and silver, sitting down by lead and spoon. And to make ready places for the other demons in which they should be confined."[32]

In modern times, demons are not known to have built anything as impressive as Solomon's temple. But people do still claim to be calling and enslaving demons. They are asking these entities for favors—and they say that the demons always deliver.

One enterprising man is so confident in his demons' performance that he actually sells them on an online auction site. The demons, which are eternally bound to metal rings, "[are focused] on protection, *your* protection. The car accident that is barely avoided, the intruder that never makes it into your home, your safety during

a storm. . . . Your demon can cause your nasty neighbor nightmares, or your ex-boss to lose his job. . . . Your demon can help you with weight loss."[33]

None of these actions will build a temple, of course. But they just might improve a person's situation in some small way. By owning an enslaved demon, people hope to bring a little bit of otherworldly power and protection into their lives.

Keeping Control

This type of protection might seem harmless enough. When it comes to evil entities, though, one cannot be too careful. People who choose to call demons take elaborate safety precautions to keep themselves safe from their unholy associates.

Many of these precautions are laid out in the *Lesser Key of Solomon*. Prior to any demon-calling ceremony, for instance, this *grimoire* advises drawing a 9-foot-wide circle (2.7m) on the floor. A pentagram, or 5-pointed star, should then be inscribed within the circle. This image is called the Circle of Salomon. A person who stands within the Circle is protected from any entities that may appear. Other images and devices specified in the *Lesser Key* have other functions, all designed to compel demons' obedience and cooperation.

In competent hands, tools and techniques like those in the *Lesser Key* are said to have great power. Still, they are not infallible. The tiniest mistake in word, deed, or even artwork can weaken a demon-summoner's spells and allow the demon to escape its bonds. When this happens, the summoner's only recourse is to invoke God's name. This desperation measure sometimes works against minor demons. Against stronger entities, unfortunately, it is seldom effective. The demon will probably break free and enter the mortal plane. Angry and offended, the entity's first deed is usually to destroy the human who invoked it.

A Healthy Respect

Mindful of this danger, some modern demon worshippers take a different approach. They are moving away from the traditional protections or, indeed, from any protections. Instead, they simply speak to demons with kindness and respect. They believe that demons will be kind and respectful to them in return.

On one Web site, a person who describes himself as a Satanist supports this viewpoint. "Using the spiritually abusive methods of the old grimoires is not only foolish, but will inevitably result in personal disaster," he explains. "Never command, demand or try to exploit [Demons] in any way. Most Demons are friendly when treated with respect."[34]

The writer says he has gotten good results using this technique. He claims that he has successfully and safely contacted many evil entities during his satanic career. Maybe this is because the writer is loyal to the devil, and the devil's demons therefore treat him well. Maybe it is because he has never actually raised a real demon, even though he believes otherwise. Or maybe, just maybe, this person has gotten incredibly lucky. He has not been harmed—yet. But one day he may make a mistake, and when that happens a demon may turn on him—possibly leading to eternal torment in the afterlife.

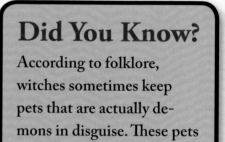

Did You Know?

According to folklore, witches sometimes keep pets that are actually demons in disguise. These pets are called "familiars."

Many people who consider themselves occult experts hold this view. Psychics, mediums, and other spiritualists tend to be wary of demons. They shy away from anything demonic, and they warn newcomers to the field to do the same. As one medium says to a rookie practitioner, "If anyone advocates summoning demons or suggests that demons are just humankind's misunderstood, maligned friends, RUN. These people have either never met a demon or are under the influence of demons as they speak. . . . Whatever you do, stay away from demons and anyone who seems to be drawn to the dark side of the occult."[35]

This seems like good advice, and most people are more than happy to heed it. After all, one does not have to believe in demons to feel a little bit nervous about them. One never knows what to expect when choosing to associate with demons.

Chapter 4

Demonic Possession

When a demon seizes control of a mortal's body and mind, it creates a condition known as demonic possession. In one well-known book on the subject, a woman named Marianne describes the moment she felt a demon take up residence in her body. At the frightful instant, Marianne recalls in a paraphrased account,

> Some tremendous pressure seemed to fall all around [her] from head to toe like a net. She shivered. And then some invisible hand seemed to have pulled a tightening cord, so that the net slipped through every inch of her body and outer self, tightening and tightening. Bit by bit "the net, now like a sharp, all surrounding hand, tightened, narrowing and narrowing all my consciousness."[36]

This "net"—which Marianne soon realized was a demon—quickly trapped its human victim in a horrific, unending nightmare. The demonic presence occupied Marianne's mind, body, and soul for years. It goaded its human host relentlessly, pushing Marianne's every thought and action toward evil.

Marianne's story is an example of demonic possession. This dread condition has been recognized in many cultures, in many different eras. Gruesome, terrifying, and sometimes even fatal, possession is the direst earthly consequence for those who dabble with demons.

A Long History

The idea of demonic possession dates back to ancient times. It probably started with shamanistic cultures, which believed that the spirits of the dead could harm the living. People who became sick or acted strangely were assumed to be under ghostly control. They could be cured only by the tribal shaman, who would contact the spirit world and persuade the attacking demon to leave its victim in peace.

Those who have witnessed demonic possession say it can lead to bizarre and sometimes frightening behavior. Dusted with ashes, covered with garlands of flowers, his tongue pierced by an iron spike, this young man from India awaits exorcism to cast out the demons that possess him.

The Real Exorcist

Father Gabriele Amorth is the most senior exorcist practicing in the Roman Catholic Church today. Amorth was ordained as a priest in 1954 and became an official exorcist in 1986. Since then, he has performed an estimated 50,000 exorcisms. Among this group, however, "only a hundred or so have been truly possessed," Amorth says.

True possession, explains Amorth, has some consistent features. Demonic victims can be identified "by their aversion to the sacrament and all things sacred. If blessed they become furious. If confronted with the crucifix, they are subdued. . . . We look into their eyes. As part of the exorcism, at specific times during the prayers, holding two fingers on the patient's eyes we raise the eyelids. Almost always, in cases of evil presence, the eyes look completely white."

A person who is possessed in this manner may do inhuman things. In one case, says Amorth, "I saw a child of 11 held down by four strong men. The child threw the men aside with ease." Another time, he recalls, "A boy of 10 lifted a huge, heavy table. Afterwards I felt the muscles in the boy's arms. He could not have done it on his own."

Some people scoff at accounts like these. They say that Amorth and others who believe in demonic possession are fanatical and deluded. Amorth does not take offense at such statements. He just smiles knowingly. "Remember, when we jeer at the Devil and tell ourselves that he does not exist, that is when he is happiest," he says.

Gyles Brandreth, "An Interview with Father Gabriele Amorth: The Church's Leading Exorcist," *Sunday Telegraph*, October 29, 2000.

The earliest written records of demonic possession come from ancient Sumeria. In this culture, all physical and mental illnesses were thought to be caused by beings called Gidim. The souls of dead people, these entities populated the Sumerian underworld. They could return to the mortal realm if they were not buried properly or given adequate offerings. When this happened, a Gidim might crawl into a human's ear and make itself at home in his or her body. The spirit could only be expelled by priests called *ashipu*, who cured sickness through elaborate ceremonies and prayers.

The dybbukim of Jewish tradition are also the spirits of the dead. These souls have been turned away from the afterlife because they have unfinished business in the mortal world. They must possess human bodies and use them to carry out their goals. Once a dybbuk gets what it wants, it may leave its host voluntarily—or it may not. In these cases, stern action is required. Certain rituals and rites can forcefully dislodge the dybbuk, which then departs the body of its human victim through the toe.

A Demon Infestation

More purely demonic than the dybbukim are the jinn of Islamic tradition. These beings have never been human, and they have no particular ties to the mortal world. Still, they are drawn to people and often infest their bodies, sometimes by the hundreds. Their hold can be loosened by various ointments and prayers. Once this is done, the human victim can expel the demons through physical force.

This expulsion process can be violent. One man who says he was possessed by hordes of jinn describes the moment the demons left his body:

> All of a sudden I felt a great surge of pressure coming out. I leaned over the bowl in front me and water began gushing out of my mouth from around the sides straight into the bowl. It kept coming out and the bowl was filling up. I couldn't believe it! I didn't even recall drinking that much water the entire day, so where was this fluid (that looked more like liquid nasal mucus) coming from? . . . I was later to discover the act of vomiting is a standard practice [that forces] the jinns to extricate involuntarily.[37]

> # Did You Know?
> According to a 2005 Gallup poll, 42 percent of U.S. residents believe in the possibility of demonic possession.

Demonic Possession in the Bible

This type of story is not unique to the Islamic tradition. Christianity, too, has its share of demon tales. Some of these tales come straight from the Bible, which includes dozens of examples of demonic possession. One of the best-known stories describes a possessed man who had supernatural strength: "He lived among the tombs; and no one could restrain him any more, even with a chain; for he had often been restrained with shackles and chains, but the chains he wrenched apart, and the shackles he broke in pieces; and no one had the strength to subdue him."[38]

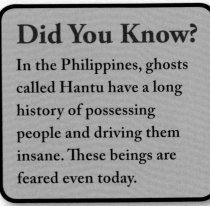

Did You Know?

In the Philippines, ghosts called Hantu have a long history of possessing people and driving them insane. These beings are feared even today.

It is no wonder this man was so strong. Not only was he possessed by a demon; it turns out that he was multiply possessed. Later in the chapter, Jesus asks for the demon's name. "My name is Legion," it replies, "for we are many."[39] This passage is the source of the Christian belief that Satan's demons, like jinn, can attack as a group. When they do, a mere human is unlikely to resist their onslaught.

Drawn to Human Hosts

If the Bible and countless other sources are to be believed, evil entities regularly seize control of people's bodies and sometimes their souls. When they do, they tend to settle in. They are very reluctant to abandon their comfortable human homes. They seem to like being human, even though mortality restricts them in some respects.

Religious scholars have come up with many explanations for this fact. One expert on Islam, for example, explains that "Jinns possess people for many reasons. Sometimes it is because the Jinn or its family has been hurt accidentally. It could be because the Jinn has fallen in love with the person. However, most of the time possession occurs because the Jinn is simply malicious and wicked."[40]

A Roman Catholic scholar agrees with the final part of this statement. He explains his feelings in an article about demonic possession.

"Evil—that is to say, evil of a demonic and personal nature—exists and constantly strives not simply to perpetuate itself, but to metastasize to anything and everything,"[41] he says. In other words, demons do not need any particular reason to possess humans. They do it because it is their nature to spread evil and because they can.

This is a lofty motivation—too lofty, say some. Many people believe that demonic possession has a very simple explanation. These people think that demons just want to live a human life for a little while. "By being in your body they can taste life, feel the sun, have a drink. That's the only way they can sample this world,"[42] explains one man. Demons will do whatever it takes to achieve this goal, which means they are always looking for people who seem vulnerable to attack.

Weaknesses Attract Demons

In most belief systems, this type of vulnerability is considered to be the result of some personal flaw. In shamanistic cultures, for instance, demons prey upon weak-minded people—those who do not have the strength of will to fight the evil forces that beset them. Shamans, on the other hand, possess unusual determination and strength of personality. These qualities allow shamans to confront and defeat demonic adversaries.

Christian tradition also states that demons attack the weak. In this tradition, however, spiritual rather than personal weakness is thought to be the key problem. People who embrace sins of any type—greed, lust, pride, anger, and the like—attract the attention of evil entities. These entities may then enter and overpower the human sinner. Faith is the only thing that is guaranteed to protect a person from this fate.

Signs and Symptoms

Not all belief systems hold this view. But most cultures agree that whatever the cause, demonic possession does happen. They also agree that possessed people do certain strange or even supernatural things. When these behaviors occur, demonic possession is strongly suspected.

A sudden change in personality is the most common sign of a demon at work. A typically happy person, for instance, might become angry and bitter overnight. A scholar might become confused, unfocused, and skeptical. A healthy person might become sick; a regular churchgoer might turn to pornography or crime; a stable person might become mentally unbalanced. All of these changes are red flags. They suggest that something—perhaps a demon?—has seized control of a human's body and is using it for unholy purposes.

A simple personality change, of course, does not prove demonic possession. Many things, including physical or mental illness, drug use, and depression, might cause such a change. To distinguish these things from true possession, the Roman Catholic Church identifies several key signs of possession. These signs include speaking in languages the individual has never learned; demonstrating impossible physical strength; seeing the future, or otherwise knowing things the person could not possibly know; and levitating or performing other supernatural feats. Above all, the possessed person loathes the names of God and Jesus. He or she experiences physical pain when confronted with prayers, religious artifacts, or other objects of faith.

A Priest's Perspective

In a 2008 article, one priest describes a case that included this entire checklist of symptoms. The subject was a woman named Julia who had asked to be evaluated for demonic possession. The evaluation took place on a warm day. Despite the weather, says the priest,

> the room . . . grew distinctly cold. Later, however, as the entity in Julia began to spout vitriol and make strange noises, members of the team felt themselves profusely sweating due to a stifling emanation of heat. . . .
>
> Multiple voices and sounds came out of [Julia]. One set consisted of loud growls and animal-like noises, which seemed to the group impossible for any human to mimic. At one point,

the voices spoke in foreign languages, including recognizable Latin and Spanish. (Julia herself only speaks English). . . .

Julia also exhibited enormous strength. Despite the religious sisters and three others holding her down with all their might, they struggled to restrain her. Remarkably, for about 30 minutes, she actually levitated about half a foot in the air. . . .

Tragedy in Romania

In early 2005 a woman named Maricica Irina Cornici entered a convent in rural Romania. Just 23 years old, Cornici was starting to display the symptoms of schizophrenia. She hoped that she could conquer her condition by dedicating her life to God.

But she never got the chance. Convent officials decided that Cornici's symptoms were signs of demonic possession. They called in an exorcist, who bound Cornici to a wooden cross in a cold room. He shoved a towel into the woman's mouth to muffle her cries. Denied food and drink, Cornici died after a three-day ordeal.

Romanian authorities arrested the priest who performed the exorcism. The priest, however, was unrepentant. "God has performed a miracle for her; finally Irina is delivered from evil," he said to the press. "I don't understand why journalists are making such a fuss about this. Exorcism is a common practice in the heart of the Romanian Orthodox church and my methods are not at all unknown to other priests."

This story highlights the dark side of exorcism. The process can allegedly deliver a possession victim from evil—but it can also kill. Whether this result means deliverance or disaster is all in the eyes of the beholder.

BBC News, "Crucified Nun Dies in 'Exorcism,'" June 18, 2005. http://news.bbc.co.uk.

The entity (or entities) that was possessing Julia, could also distinguish between holy water and regular water. She would scream in pain when the blessed water was sprinkled upon her, but have no reaction to clandestine use of unblessed water. During the ceremonies, she also revealed hidden or past events in the lives of the various attendees, including information about deceased relatives completely unknown to her.[43]

This account seems extraordinary. But surprisingly, it is far from unique. Thousands of stories like this one exist. These stories have been written by many different types of people: religious officials, observers, interviewers, mental health professionals, family members, and even the possessed themselves. They all claim to describe actual cases of demonic possession.

The Strange Case of Robbie Mannheim

Of these stories, the case of "Robbie Mannheim" (a pseudonym) may be the best known. Robbie was a regular boy from a middle-class family, living in a quiet Maryland town. Friends remember him as a bit of a troublemaker, but Robbie's mischief was standard teenage fare. The youth did not seem especially troubled, and he certainly did not have an unusual interest in demons.

One day in January 1949, however, Robbie and his aunt experimented with a Ouija board. A series of odd events soon followed. Robbie's family started to hear dripping and scratching sounds within the walls of their house. Pictures of Jesus fell off the walls. At night, Robbie's bed squeaked and shook inexplicably, and claw marks appeared on his mattress. A few weeks later, the claw marks turned up on Robbie's body. Some of the marks seemed to spell messages.

> **Did You Know?**
>
> Christianity identifies a condition called demonic oppression. In this condition, which can last for years, demons are attacking a human but have not yet seized control of his or her body.

At this point, Robbie's family became worried enough to summon a team of priests. The priests agreed to evaluate the boy for possession. When they did, they saw some things that seemed to have no earthly explanation. Father Raymond Bishop writes in a diary that he witnessed Robbie's mattress shaking and that he saw scratches appear on the boy's body. Another priest, Father Halloran, saw the scratches as well. He also witnessed objects moving on their own. "I saw a bottle slide from a dresser across the room—there was no one near it,"[44] he recalls in a 1999 interview.

Keeping the Story Alive

These things convinced the priests that Robbie was indeed a genuine victim of demonic possession. They assembled a team to expel Robbie's demon through prayer and ritual. This simple process turned out to have an extreme effect on Robbie's behavior. During the ritual, the boy screamed curses and vulgarities at the priests, sometimes in Latin. He vomited and urinated almost continually. At one point Robbie reportedly grabbed a bedspring, snapped the thick metal like a twig, and stabbed a priest's arm with the object's jagged end. At another point, a portrait of the devil, seemingly drawn in blood, appeared on Robbie's calf.

None of these things dissuaded the priests. They continued their ritual no matter what Robbie said or did—and after many hours, their persistence paid off. Robbie's body spasmed violently, then relaxed for the first time since the ceremony had begun. Robbie sat up in his bed and looked wonderingly at the priests. "He is gone,"[45] the boy said.

Robbie's troubles may have been over. The public's fascination with demonic possession, however, was about to explode. William Peter Blatty, a student at nearby Georgetown University, heard about the Mannheim incident, and he eventually wrote a novel based on Robbie's tale. Called *The Exorcist*, Blatty's novel was an immediate hit upon its publication in 1971. The movie version of this book, also called *The Exorcist*, was released in 1973. Graphic, disturbing, and downright disgusting, this film is a classic of the horror genre. It is considered to be one of the scariest movies ever made.

The 1973 movie The Exorcist *presented a graphic, disturbing view of a young girl possessed by a demon and the efforts required to exorcise that demon. Actress Linda Blair appears here in a scene from the movie.*

Casting Out the Demon

It may also be one of the most sensationalized. *The Exorcist* is undeniably exciting, but demon experts say that it is highly exaggerated as well. In its danger and drama, this film puts a classic Hollywood spin on the casting out of demons.

Most real exorcisms, according to those who conduct them, are not so harrowing. In Christian tradition, these rites usually involve one or more exorcists praying over a possessed person and commanding the demon to leave. The prayers are repeated over and over, sometimes for weeks on end. Supernatural occurrences are few and far between during the exorcism period, and indeed, they may not happen at all. In most cases, exorcists see no sure signs of demonic activity.

But sometimes they do see unusual things, like those that occurred during the exorcism of Robbie Mannheim. When this is the case, faith becomes the exorcist's most powerful weapon. The Islamic exorcist calls upon Allah to vanquish the invading entity; the Christian exorcist seeks help from God, Jesus, the Holy Ghost, or various saints; and exorcists of other faiths petition their own particular protectors. By invoking these names, the exorcist asks for divine help in terrifying the demon and loosening its hold.

Prayers and Rituals

Of all major belief systems, Roman Catholicism probably has the most specific exorcism process. This process is laid out word for word in a church publication called the *Roman Ritual*. To successfully vanquish a demon, the exorcist must recite the ritual's many prayers exactly as they are written. One typical prayer reads:

> I cast you out, unclean spirit, along with every Satanic power of the enemy, every spectre from hell, and all your fell companions; in the name of our Lord Jesus Christ. Begone and stay far from this creature of God. For it is He who commands you, He who flung you headlong from the heights of heaven into the depths of hell. It is He who commands you, He who once stilled the sea and the wind and the storm. Hearken, therefore, and tremble in fear, Satan. . . . Begone, then, in the name of the Father, and of the Son, and of the Holy Ghost. . . . Amen.[46]

This prayer and others like it can have great power. But these weapons cannot be used by just anybody. Demon experts warn that exorcism prayers and rituals are worthless and possibly even dangerous in the wrong hands. One self-described shaman addresses this concept from a non-Christian viewpoint when he says, "Someone who undertakes [an exorcism] and has failed to prepare and train fully for it will in most cases be severely disabled, maddened or otherwise left far less than they were before attempting the techniques."[47] According to this man and many others, casting out demons is perilous work indeed.

Is Demonic Possession Real?

It is also, they say, very real. Most exorcists are absolutely certain that they are doing battle with evil. They feel this way not because they have faith but because of the inexplicable things they see and experience during the exorcism process. Psychiatrist and writer M. Scott Peck, who has participated in several exorcisms, was initially skeptical but ended up changing his mind. "I had been converted . . . from a belief that the Devil did not exist to a belief—a certainty—that the Devil does exist and probably demons (under the control of the Devil) as well,"[48] he says.

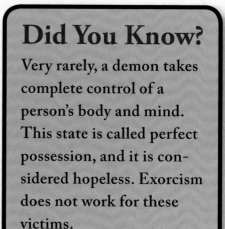

Did You Know?

Very rarely, a demon takes complete control of a person's body and mind. This state is called perfect possession, and it is considered hopeless. Exorcism does not work for these victims.

To support this statement, Peck describes the exorcism of a woman named Beccah. During the procedure, Beccah underwent an extraordinary change. "She did not appear to be a human being at all. To everyone present, her entire face became like that of a snake,"[49] he says. This change did not show up on a video recording of the exorcism, but Peck is absolutely convinced that it occurred. The team's experience of Beccah as a snake, he says, was unanimous.

Peck may be a believer. People who have not come face-to-face with demons, however, are not usually so sure. Many people believe that alleged possession cases are actually caused by mental illness. They place the blame on conditions such as schizophrenia, which causes hallucinations, disordered thinking, and other disturbing symptoms. A disorder called Tourette's syndrome is also mentioned frequently in connection with demonic possession. This condition causes jerky movements and obscene vocal outbursts that are sometimes thought to be the work of demons.

Some possession victims, suggest disbelievers, do not even have the excuse of mental illness to explain their behavior. They are simply faking it. People who hold this opinion point out that anyone can scream obscenities, thrash around wildly, and pretend to be repelled by religious artifacts. They think that a good actor, pretending to be

A young man, age 24, undergoes an exorcism in Mexico City. During the ritual, which lasted almost four hours, the young man kicked, screamed, and spit blood but also calmly talked and prayed. Exorcists say demons fully reveal themselves during such rituals.

possessed by a demonic entity, can easily deceive an exorcist—who is, after all, already inclined toward belief.

Most religious organizations walk the line between these extremes of belief. Officials admit that most "possession" victims are just disturbed or sick. Exorcists are therefore instructed to look for mental illness, physical disorders, or outright fakery before considering possession. In almost all cases, these things are found. The exorcist sends the client to the appropriate professional rather than performing the ritual of exorcism.

Seeing Is Believing

Every now and then, however, the exorcist comes across a case where something feels different. This "something" can be as simple as an odd look in the patient's eyes or an unusual tone of voice. Whatever it is, the exorcist starts to suspect that a demon is present. He or she undertakes an exorcism—and this is when the truth becomes apparent. For it is only during the exorcism process, exorcists say, that demons fully reveal themselves.

> ## Did You Know?
> Many church-sanctioned exorcists are currently working within the Roman Catholic Church. The exact number is not public, but it is thought to exceed 400.

Believers say that this fact is responsible for the general public's skepticism about demonic possession. People do not believe what they do not see with their own eyes. But exorcists have seen it all. As a result, their belief is strong. Father Halloran, the priest who assisted at Robbie Mannheim's exorcism, recalls something another participant told him. "[The church] will never say whether it was or it wasn't a genuine exorcism," the priest said to Halloran, "but you know it and I know it. We were there."[50]

These men will be forever convinced by what they saw. They will continue to fight demonic intrusions into the human world.

Other people will maintain their skepticism, believing that demons are movie monsters and nothing more. The matter may never be proved one way or another. But when it comes to demons, at least one thing is certain: They can always be counted on to give people a good scare. In reality or in nightmares, these beings will continue to terrorize humankind just as they have already done for thousands of years.

Source Notes

Introduction: What Is a Demon?

1. Quoted in Laura Knight-Jadczyk, "Alien Abduction, Demonic Possession, and the Legend of the Vampire," Cassiopaean Experiment, 1994. www.cassiopaea.org.

Chapter One: Demons in World Mythology

2. Donald Tyson, "The Truth About Demons," Donald Tyson's Supernatural World. www.donaldtyson.com.
3. Swami Nirmalananda Giri, trans., Bhagavad Gita, 16: 7, 9–10. Atma Jyoti Ashram, 2004. www.atmajyoti.org.
4. *Thaindian News*, "Tribal Body in Madhya Pradesh Issues Directive to Worship Ravana," October 6, 2008. www.thaindian.com.
5. ReligionFacts, "Ghosts, Spirits and Demons," February 3, 2005. www.religionfacts.com.
6. M.M. Pickthall, trans., Qur'an 72:11, 14–15. www.sacred-texts.com.
7. Judika Illes, *Encyclopedia of Spirits*. New York: HarperOne, 2009, pp. 129–30.
8. Quoted in James F. Downs, *Washo Religion*. Berkeley and Los Angeles: University of California Press, 1961, p. 13. www.gutenberg.org.
9. Andrew Munroe, "Caribbean Stories," Caribbean Folklore, May 13, 2008. caribbeanfolklore.net.

Chapter Two: Demons in Charge

10. *Encyclopedia Britannica*, 11th ed., s.v. "Demonology."
11. The Wanderling, "Mara," Awakening 101. the-wanderling.com.
12. Quoted in Barbara O'Brien, "Mara, Lord of Death: The Demon Who Challenged the Buddha," About.com Buddhism. buddhism.about.com.
13. Museo del Templo Mayor, "Mictlantecuhtli and the World of the Dead," Archaeological Research Institute, Arizona State University, November 30, 2000. http://archaeology.la.asu.edu.

14. Museo del Templo Mayor, "Mictlantecuhtli and the World of the Dead."

15. Pickthall, Qur'an 7:11–13.

16. *Jewish Encyclopedia*, 1st ed., s.v. "Asmodeus."

17. Isaiah 14:13–14 (King James Version).

18. Revelations 12:7–9 (King James Version).

19. Exposing Satanism, "Satan's Origin." www.exposingsatanism. org.

20. S.E. Schlosser, "Dancing with the Devil: A Texas Ghost Story," American Folkore. http://americanfolklore.net.

21. S.E. Schlosser, "The Devil's Hole: A French Canadian Folktale," American Folklore. http://americanfolklore.net.

Chapter Three: Associating with Demons

22. Illes, *Encyclopedia of Spirits*, p. 21.

23. Illes, *Encyclopedia of Spirits*, p. 21.

24. Mark, "Terrorized by a Demonic Spirit," About.com Paranormal, March 2004. http://paranormal.about.com.

25. Mark, "Terrorized by a Demonic Spirit."

26. Callista, "Battle with a Demon," About.com Paranormal, November 2004. http://paranormal.about.com.

27. Darren, "A Warning to Ouija Users," Your Ghost Stories, March 23, 2009. www.yourghoststories.com.

28. BadJuuJuu, comment following "My Gran's Ouija Board Experience," Your Ghost Stories, July 1, 2010. www.yourghoststories. com.

29. Quoted in Ontario Consultants on Religious Tolerance, "Is Demonic Possession and Exorcism Still Valid?" Religious Tolerance, October 21, 2004. www.religioustolerance.org.

30. Quoted in Ontario Consultants on Religious Tolerance, "Is Demonic Possession and Exorcism Still Valid?"

31. *The Grand Grimoire, or the Art of Commanding Heavenly Spirits.* Paris: n.p., 1845, pp. 26–27. www.scribd.com.

32. Quoted in *Jewish Quarterly Review*, "The Testament of Solomon," trans. F.C. Conybeare, October 1898; digital edition by Joseph H. Peterson, Esoteric Archives, 1997. www.esoteric archives.com.

33. Black Wolf, "Demonology 101," Demons Rule 666. www.demons rule666.com.

34. Quoted in Joy of Satan Ministries, "How to Summon Demons." www.angelfire.com.

35. Julia Melges-Brenner, "Natural Medium Is Dabbling in the Occult," Muse-Net, February 4, 2008. www.muse-net.com.

Chapter Four: Demonic Possession

36. Malachi Martin, *Hostage to the Devil: The Possession and Exorcism of Five Contemporary Americans*. New York: Reader's Digest, 1976. www.scribd.com.

37. The Truth About Spontaneous Chi Kung, "My Story: An Experience of Jinn Possession." www.dangerofchi.org.

38. Mark 5:3–4 (New Revised Standard Version).

39. Mark 5:9 (New Revised Standard Version).

40. Islam Awareness, "The World of Jinn," *Invitation to Islam*, no. 4, January 1998. www.islamawareness.net.

41. Geoffrey K. Mondello, "The Exorcist: Priesthood at the Door of Darkness," *Boston Catholic Journal*. www.boston-catholic-journal. com.

42. Timothy, "Demon Possession: A Candid Conversation," True Ghost Tales, 2008. www.trueghosttales.com.

43. Quoted in Richard E. Gallagher, "Among the Many Counterfeits: A Case of Demonic Possession," *New Oxford Review*, March 30, 2008. catholiccitizens.org.

44. Quoted in Mark Opsasnick, "The Haunted Boy of Cottage City," *Strange Magazine*, 1999. www.strangemag.com.

45. Quoted in Opsasnick, "The Haunted Boy of Cottage City."

46. Life Enterprises Unlimited, "Rite for Exorcism," *Roman Ritual*, ch. 2. www.trosch.org.

47. Craig Berry, "Dispossessions," On Mind, Matter, Energy, Space & Spirit. www.craigberry.net.

48. M. Scott Peck, *Glimpses of the Devil*. New York: Free Press, 2005, p. 238.

49. Peck, *Glimpses of the Devil*, p. 173.

50. Quoted in Propheties On Line, "Casting Out the Devil." www. propheties.it.

For Further Exploration

Books

Gabriele Amorth, *An Exorcist Tells His Story*. San Francisco: Ignatius, 1999.

Harold Bloom, *Bloom's Major Literary Characters: Satan*. Philadelphia: Chelsea House, 2005.

Katie Boyd, *Devils & Demonology in the 21st Century*. Atglen, PA: Schiffer, 2009.

Rosemary Ellen Gulley, *The Encyclopedia of Demons and Demonology*. New York: Facts On File, 2009.

Stoker Hunt, *Ouija: The Most Dangerous Game*. New York: Barnes & Noble, 1992.

David E. Jones, *Evil in Our Midst: A Chilling Glimpse of Our Most Feared and Frightening Demons*. Garden City Park, NY: Square One, 2002.

Donna Jo Napoli, *The Wager*. New York: Henry Holt, 2010.

Bulbul Sharma, *Tales of Fabled Beasts, Gods, and Demons*. New York: Viking, 2003.

Tracy Wilkinson, *The Vatican's Exorcists: Driving Out the Devil in the 21st Century*. New York: Warner, 2007.

Web Sites

American Association of Exorcists (aaeok.tripod.com). This site contains a wealth of information for anyone who wants to find or become an exorcist.

The Exorcist Fansite (captainhowdy.com). This site include anything and everything concerning the *Exorcist* film series, including film clips, plot summaries, news links, message boards, and much more.

God Checker (www.godchecker.com). This site profiles over 3,700 other-worldly beings, including the demons of many different cultures.

Internet Sacred Text Archive (www.sacred-texts.com). This is the Web's largest free archive of books about religion, mythology, folklore, and the esoteric. It contains many demonic works, including the full texts of many *grimoires*.

Monstrous (www.monstrous.com). This site has extensive information on every imaginable monster, including demons.

Index

Picture Credits

About the Author

Kris Hirschmann has written more than 200 books for children. She owns and runs a business that provides a variety of writing and editorial services. She lives near Orlando, Florida, with her husband, Michael, and her daughters, Nikki and Erika.